Animals That Live in the Ocean

Octopuses and Squids

By Valerie J. Weber

Reading Consultant: Susan Nations, M.Ed.,
author/literacy coach/consultant in literacy development

WEEKLY READER®
PUBLISHING

Please visit our web site at www.garethstevens.com.
For a free catalog describing our list of high-quality books,
call 1-800-542-2595 (USA) or 1-800-387-3178 (Canada).
Our fax: 1-877-542-2596

Library of Congress Cataloging-in-Publication Data
Weber, Valerie.
   Octopuses and squids / by Valerie J. Weber.
      p. cm. — (Animals that live in the ocean)
   Includes bibliographical references and index.
   ISBN-10: 0-8368-9242-9 ISBN-13: 978-0-8368-9242-0 (lib. bdg.)
   ISBN-10: 0-8368-9341-7 ISBN-13: 978-0-8368-9341-0 (softcover)
   1. Octopuses—Juvenile literature. 2. Squids—Juvenile literature.
 I. Title.
 QL430.3.O2W43 2009
 594'.56—dc22   2008014498

This edition first published in 2009 by
Weekly Reader® Books
An Imprint of Gareth Stevens Publishing
1 Reader's Digest Road
Pleasantville, NY 10570-7000 USA

Senior Managing Editor: Lisa M. Herrington
Senior Editor: Barbara Bakowski
Creative Director: Lisa Donovan
Designer: Alexandria Davis
Cover Designer: Amelia Favazza, *Studio Montage*
Photo Researcher: Diane Laska-Swanke

Photo Credits: Cover, pp. 1, 5, 7, 11, 15 (both), 17, 19, 21 © SeaPics.com;
p. 9 © Jorgen Jessen/AFP/Getty Images; p. 13 © Jeff Rotman/Alamy

Printed in the United States of America

1 2 3 4 5 6 7 8 9 10 09 08

Table of Contents

Boldface words appear in the glossary.

Armed for the Deep Sea

An octopus creeps along the ocean floor. It sneaks up on a snail. Suddenly, eight arms dart forward. The octopus pulls the snail to its mouth.

octopus

snail

An octopus looks like a floppy balloon with eight arms. The balloon is the main part of the octopus's body. It is called the **mantle**.

mantle

eight arms

Below the mantle is the octopus's head. It has two large eyes and a brain. Octopuses are smart. They can twist open jars and even solve puzzles!

jar

A web of skin stretches between the octopus's arms. Round **suckers** line the bottom of each arm. The octopus can use its suckers to stick to rocks.

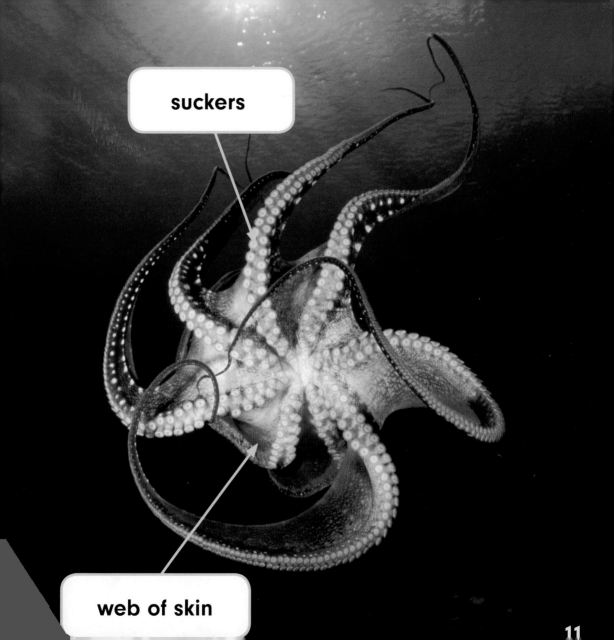

suckers

web of skin

Octopuses and squids belong to the same group of sea animals. Like octopuses, squids have eight arms. Squids also have two longer **tentacles** to help them catch food.

two tentacles

A Show of Colors

Both squids and octopuses can change colors quickly. They sometimes change colors to warn other animals to stay away.

before color change

after color change

Squids and octopuses change colors to hide from enemies, too. They can blend into the seafloor. Can you spot the octopus?

A Quick Escape

Squids and octopuses squirt a cloud of ink to confuse enemies. The ink cloud is the same size as the squid or octopus. An enemy cannot tell what to attack!

ink

Octopuses and squids squirt water, too. They shoot out a jet of water through a special tube. The blast of water pushes the animal away from danger.

tube

Glossary

mantle: the main part of a squid's or an octopus's body

suckers: body parts used for sticking to something

tentacles: long, thin, flexible structures that stick out from the head of a squid

For More Information

Books

Octopus. Rourke Discovery Library (series).
Lynn M. Stone (Rourke Publishing, 2005)

Squids. Weird Wonders of the Deep (series).
Valerie J. Weber (Gareth Stevens Publishing, 2005)

Web Sites

Monterey Bay Aquarium: Giant Octopus
www.montereybayaquarium.org/efc/octopus.asp
Learn about the giant octopus and watch one being fed.

Squids at Enchanted Learning
www.enchantedlearning.com/subjects/invertebrates/squid/Squidprintout.shtml
Color in a diagram of a squid and learn more about its body.

Publisher's note to educators and parents: Our editors have carefully reviewed these web sites to ensure that they are suitable for children. Many web sites change frequently, however, and we cannot guarantee that a site's future contents will continue to meet our high standards of quality and educational value. Be advised that children should be closely supervised whenever they access the Internet.

Index

About the Author

A writer and editor for 25 years, Valerie Weber especially loves working in children's publishing. The variety of topics is endless, from weird animals to making movies. It is her privilege to try to engage children in their world through books.